Between Two Gardens

Between Two Gardens

Poems

Laura Quinn Guidry

ALAMO BAY PRESS
SEADRIFT•AUSTIN

Copyright © 2017 by Laura Quinn Guidry

All rights reserved. No part of this book may be reproduced in any form without permission in writing from the publisher, except by a reviewer who may quote brief passages in a review.

Cover illustration: LRG Photography
Book Design: ABP

For orders and information:
Alamo Bay Press
Pamela Booton, Director
825 W 11th Ste 114
Austin, Texas 78701
pam@alamobaypress.com
www.alamobaypress.com

Library of Congress Control Number: 2016963829
ISBN: 978-1-943306-05-3

For Koren

...Take your practiced strengths and stretch them
   until they reach between two
   contradictions...For far inside you
   the god wishes to consult.

   —Rilke

Contents

            I

1   Listening
2   Rush
3   Flight
4   Fishing with My Father
6   So Damn Hot
7   That Little Girl
8   Red
9   Love Poem
10 Watching MTV with My Son
11 Back Home
12 Baptism
13 Civil Disobedience
14 Light and Shadows
15 Losses
16 Mother Oaks
18 April 19
19 Cold Night
20 Before Dawn
21 Wings
22 Alone

            II

25 Morning
26 Skin
27 Living a Line from T. S. Eliot
28 The Fawn
29 Our Daughter's Dog

30	Real
31	Calves
32	Sunday Afternoon in Texas
33	A Handout
34	Full Moon in Transom
35	The Snarl
36	Thirst
37	Under a Full Moon
38	Visitor
39	Doors
40	Sign of Contradiction
42	Flash Flood
43	His Dog
44	Flavor
45	Tommy
46	A Few Words
47	Reckoning the Earth

III

51	Incandescent
53	Bird of Many Colors
54	Familiar
55	Of Home
56	Sunset on the River from the 16th Floor
57	Of the Grandfather I Barely Knew
58	Friday
59	Heron
60	The Prairie Iris
61	Between Two Gardens
62	The Hum
63	Mimicry

64 Turning
65 Frogs at the Robert Frost Farm
66 At Breakfast
67 Matrix
71 A Song for Listeners

73 Thanks
75 Acknowledgments
77 About Laura Quinn Guidry

Between Two Gardens

I

Listening

I have listened to the night.
The many-layered,
impenetrable quiet.

The lull in my son's old room.
He had just moved out —
young, eager. In sleep,
defenseless against death.

Only in dreams now
will a child's sweet voice
summon me awake.

From far away, undertones
of a train, faint enough
to have you doubt the truth of it.

My daughter moves back
home for awhile.
A first love ending.
A mending of lives.

This morning, through the wall
between our rooms,
I hear her speaking to her dog.
I can't make out the words,

but the lilt of her voice
reaches the stilled places
where silence leans toward
the timbre of devotion.

Rush

It sprang forth at sundown and was gone—
flash of dark motion, leggy,
black winding stripe of a tail—
so fast I couldn't see its face
only the red-brown blur of its body.

Now, at the place on the road
where the bobcat leapt
I slow down and look
each time I pass
hoping to see it again or another.

I come to the country, I say,
for the unhurried pace and the solitude.
But, sometimes,
there is a bolt of life so unexpected,
so intoxicating

that I think
this is what propels me.
This and, then, desire for a better look.

Laura Quinn Guidry

Flight

She begs him not to let the bird go.
A house bird, a cage bird
a little, dew-grass green bird.
The wild birds will kill it.
All the while she argues
the child finds an oblong leaf
makes it swoop and soar
and sails beneath it.
And the child, the leaf
and the yellow-dawn bird
vanish into sky.

Fishing with My Father

on Bayou Boeuf forty years ago
before the duckweed took over.
Daddy paddles the boat.
I sit with a cane pole and bait can,

sliding worms onto a hook,
their bodies oozing earth from the chicken yard.
The ritual digging late the day before.
My knowing the best places.

Shorty, my father's old fishing buddy,
once dubbed me "the best worm-digger
in Rapides Parish." Daddy liked to tell that.
It was easy to please him then.

He guides the boat
through the shallows near the bank.
Cypress cast cool shadows on the water,
shade where fish were apt to bite.

A branch hangs low.
"Careful how you fling that line.
Don't need any squirrel-fishing today."
He liked to say that.

Up a ways, a moccasin slides off the bank.
Nearby, turtles sun themselves on a log.
My father taught me how to tell the tug
of a turtle on the line.

"A turtle holds the cork under longer.
Swallows it all—bait and hook.
Have to cut its head off.
Best to avoid that."

Laura Quinn Guidry

Midstream, our little boat drifts.
Stillness all around us.
I learned to love the quiet, there, on the water
with my father. Water falling in soft plops
from the paddle. Each drop, a circle widening.

Once, he told me what he'd always wanted
to do in life. And once, years later, he said,
"I always thought *you'd* be a writer,"
(but only after he thought I'd missed the chance.)

The cork bobbles halfheartedly.
The flash of a sun perch close to the surface.
A dragonfly lighting on the line,
its windowpane wings veined with silver.

Some days contain a world.
We are given what we need.
Our claiming comes later
in writing our lives.

So Damn Hot

In New Orleans, in the fifties
we barely slept through the swelter
of summer. Subdivision houses sat
with open windows on trimmed lawns.
The people who lived next door

were Irish like us. Only not like us.
"Shanty Irish" my father called them.
On weekends in their enclosed carport
they played poker with friends, drank beer
and cursed. Expletives flew out

those jalousie windows.
(My parents drank cocktails nightly,
played Mantovani and never cursed.)
My sister and I lay sweaty in our twin beds,
the window raised, our room

closest to the noisy carport.
Once my father went over there,
told them his young daughters
were not accustomed to hearing swearing.
They paid no mind.

In those summers, when it was so damn hot,
heat stifled sleep, words could startle
the stillness, penetrate our filmy curtains,
linger long enough for me
to marvel at them.

That Little Girl

At the cemetery in August
parched grass and dulled bronze.
Our son would be thirty-two today.
We spend the afternoon in mindless errands,
eat supper at a Mexican restaurant
too tired to cook.

In the Ladies' Room,
a girl, nine or so, freckles,
sandy hair cropped like a boy's,
all arms, legs and motion.
"Wash up to your elbows,"
her mother insists on the way out.
"Get the grit off."

She dunks elbows in the sink,
splashes out, jumps up
to pull down the paper towel.
Again, each jump higher than before.
The room resounds
with the clatter of the dispenser
her feet on the floor.

She stops to watch me put on lipstick.
"Earth Red" the shade.
An abrupt quiet.
Her curious blue eyes.
"You look pretty today," she says.

Red

We called them mosquito hawks as children
and caught them when we could.
They had the advantage —
wraparound eyes, two pairs of wings.
Not content to admire their aerial acrobatics
we grabbed those glittering wings
even if we had to tear them.
Iridescent blue green insects, magical
like fireflies we imprisoned in jars.

This afternoon a red dragonfly
lights on a coneflower, a faded cone
on a long stem, purple petals gone.
I've never seen a red dragonfly before.
Its red is not the red of the cardinals fighting.
I want to capture that actual shade of red
but words like pinkish-red or rosy feel as clumsy
as fingers grasping wings.

Love Poem

My husband is driving
his tractor on the side of the hill.
Only his head and shoulders are visible,

his wide-brimmed hat.
He is fifty-four
and the sun has become unfriendly.

He cuts the wheel sharply.
The tractor bumps along the ridge.
He is the boy

in the photograph on the bookshelf
standing tall
on the pedals of his bike.

My husband disappears
down the hill.
The boy pumps the pedals hard.

He'll pop wheelies, cut figure eights
and ride the wind home at nightfall —
breathless, hungry.

Watching MTV with My Son

I can see him
lounging in the armchair
loafers in their kicked-off place on the floor
sports section strewn there, too
a super-sized plastic cup in a watery
ring on the console table.
We are watching Clapton Unplugged,
"Tears in Heaven" —
a song of unimaginable loss —
and remarking, *lovely song, so sad.*

Back Home

Hours after the funeral, the house slowly empties.
All afternoon I've thought
Grant would want to be here
among the people he loved and all this good food.

Our aunt and uncle from New Orleans
ladling bowls of oyster artichoke soup,
serving up warm bread pudding with whiskey sauce.
Who will refute the brief comfort of food from home?

I sit with my daughter on the sofa.
Koren is twenty and beautiful.
Dark hair in a new cut.
Pixie, we used to call it. It becomes her.

In the kitchen, my mother-in-law puts up the food.
To the last people here
she offers some to take home.
More than we need, she tells them.

Koren and I speak low.
We've had to do the hardest things.
We needed everyone to be here.
We need them to go home.

Baptism

The week the hurricane
immersed New Orleans
witnessed a dissolution
as if my history there
had been washed away —
abandoning all but the spirit
of a young life.
Even memory is permeable,
the water discloses.

Civil Disobedience

My parents had forbidden
the French Quarter after school.

Their instructions: Take the streetcar
to Canal Street, board the bus for home.

No detours.
It was 1965 and I was sixteen.

After a quick trip to the Acorn Shop—
incense and all things bohemian—

I cut in front of the Wildlife
and Fisheries building on Royal Street

where dissenters were demonstrating.
I don't recall the point of their protest

but I do remember what I was wearing—
striped turtleneck, mini skirt,

white go-go boots, Sassoon haircut.
I remember my inability to protest

the next morning when my parents
recounted the French Quarter fracas

broadcast on the ten o'clock news.
A peaceful picket had turned to

pushing, shoving and falling placards
and, in the midst, their daughter

caught on camera—smoking, too—
displayed for all the world to see.

Light and Shadows

On the ceiling of my room in the old hotel
the city comes back in shadow,
in louvered light.

Street light, filtered through small-slatted
shutters, bends where wall and ceiling meet
and evokes ferns, tipped, beckoning.

Neon lights and a flashing star from the casino
next door make a garish montage
of purple, pink, teal and silver.

Light from a streetcar shifts
into an image of vertebrae, a ladder
or a track running under a train.

I've come back to New Orleans
to visit an old friend who is dying.
The family I had here is gone.

This hotel's restaurant, where we used
to celebrate, gone, but its towering dessert
Mile High Pie available by room service.

Earlier I ordered one and savored each bite
looking out on St. Charles Avenue
to the white church with four spires.

Beyond the church, the river and bridge
constant and reassuring.
In the dark the bridge links heaven and earth

by a strand of golden beads. Above me
chandelier prisms scintillate. It is near midnight.
Enough of ceiling skeletons.

Tomorrow is a day I can't get back.

Laura Quinn Guidry

Losses

I've run out of places
  to store my losses.
No more cubbyholes
  to tuck them into.
No compartments
  to keep them
until I'm ready
  to release them
in small measures.

Here's another.
Unexpected
incremental
sorrow
confronts me,
rouses the others.
Now they won't keep quiet.
Now they won't stay put.

And I,
reluctant Pandora,
must let them out
  to move about
and have their say.

Mother Oaks

    A sad lot, these Texas blackjack oaks
shaped by torsion of wind, scorches of sun,
stretches of deprivation. Competing with yaupon
and cedars for meagerness, they dispatch
roots into rock, breaking up caliche,
delving deeper for water.

    Poor twisted trees, you are not the mother oaks
of my girlhood, gracious live oaks sprawling
across St. Augustine lawns in New Orleans.
And where is the one I loved on Rosalie Plantation?
Towering forty feet, spreading fifty,
limbs, on one side, stretched into the bull pen
and, on the other, shaded the kitchen
where Grandma and Mama cooked.

    A cathedral of a tree and I, its priestess.
A castle and I, its maiden.
Spending hours among the exposed roots,
I filled furrows with water, made dough
which I baked in a cement-block oven,
served with tea from a china blue pot.

    All gone now; the farm sold.
Once my sister and I went back, stood
at the cattle gap, looked up the long drive
at the house with its new facade, signs that said
Private. Later we learned the owner was killed
when he got between a cow and her calf.

    I am the age of my mother when she died.
January, June, December — my grandmother
buried husband, son, daughter.
My own son dead now.
And I am here among these inelegant trees

Laura Quinn Guidry

with their noisy leaves, falling leaves;
here, bare-boned, belonging, living close
to the hardscrabble earth, reaching way down
just to keep on living.

April 19

From Lake Mexia, a mound of earth rises.
Trees lifting fleshless limbs line the highway.
I'm taking a roundabout route
to a writers' conference in Waco,
happening upon this strange place.
Some ancient shift of earth.

It is March but I'm remembering
that day in April
when at work we kept the radio tuned
to news of the cataclysm
two hundred miles north in Waco
when after work at the car wash
strangers exchanged shock and dismay
when later that same day I would learn
my son in his apartment
had not answered phone calls
or knocks at the door,
had not awakened or arisen
      when night would descend upon day
when on the same day two years later
in Oklahoma, children would die
in an exploding building
and public and private grief again embrace.

Now, all these years later, I'm
traveling with unseen companions
through this looming place,
this luring place of heaped earth,
trees beseeching sky.

Laura Quinn Guidry

Cold Night

The cedars, thick and darker than the sky.
A deliberate wind stirs them.
It is October. The first cold night.
I cannot sleep, remembering
when he was little and I dressed him
to keep the cold out.

Knit cap pulled snug.
Small fingers into gloves.
Parka zipped and neatly tied.
Years later, jacket slung
over a shoulder, he'd look back,
give me a smile to pacify.

It is not right to be here
under blanket and comforter
when he lies in clay-cold earth.
Only the wind is honest
in the rasp and clank of loosened tin,
the hollow whine in the chimney.

Before Dawn

The voices of the coyotes come,
not from the deep woods now
but from the fence line.
Unless the wind deceives, carrying
their sharp barks and giddy trills closer.
The hour is morning, although still dark.

In another hour, light will rise
over the open range.
Cold air will contain the whistles
of titmice and churrs of house wrens,
the distant cawing of crows
and lowing of cattle.

Wind will have scattered
the night's wails.

Wings

I wave to my daughter
as she sits up high in the truck
her fiancé is driving,
all her belongings in back.
Soon they'll be setting up house
in a Midwestern state
I've never set foot in.
She smiles and waves.

I recall the saying on the plaque
that hung on the kitchen wall
when Koren and Grant were
little and I was young.
The one about parents and children.
The one about roots and wings.

Alone

Toward evening I travel
past ranches and small farms.
Alone in a field, a cow
eats the scant grass. Behind her,
dense trees curve away.

You know how it is when
just as you pass something
it catches your eye
and, then, in your mind's eye
you see it again?

It was as if all loneliness
lived in that one unremarkable cow
in her little field
her head lowered and night
already in the trees.

Laura Quinn Guidry

II

Morning

I'll admit
sometimes it's not the world
I love
so much as the thought of it.

First, the constant hum of crickets.
A vibration.
Then a bird or two.
A twitter, a chirp.
Light eases through the trees.
The trees not black or green exactly.
The sky not white or blue.
A gradation.

Sitting on the screened porch,
not quite outside or in.
The long hour between ending and beginning.
A limbo place where I wait
for color to come back
chatter to become song.

Skin

He shows me the snake skin
in the low limbs of the yaupon holly
draped over branches
the way a shawl might fall
across a woman's shoulders, might slip
to one side and dangle.
Cool rub of raw silk.
The tree had clutched and tugged.
Skin past resisting, scored, striated
the color of age —
It isn't easy to release the self
that's felt the world,
to let thorns assist.

Probably only a ribbon snake
like the one we came upon last spring
among rocks and damp mulch.
Startling — a flash (that's all you get)
to remember the sound
as it slid over stone.
Dark curve of morning, blood-red
and yellowing light.

Laura Quinn Guidry

Living a Line from T. S. Eliot

April comes around again
fertile and immediate
to deliver her commemoration.
We honor our son with flowers —
cut stems of numbered days —
while earth flaunts her brilliance
her burgeoning life.

The Fawn

At dusk, a fawn slips under
a barbed-wire fence, wanders
onto a country road.
We stop the car and wait.
No other cars come.

Ears pricked, the fawn listens.
Huge black eyes stare
at the car for the longest time.
Trying to make
sense of the world.
Too innocent to be wary.

The fawn takes a step back,
stops, then a step forward.
Spindle-legged, it could
topple at any moment.
Life is slender.

Laura Quinn Guidry

Our Daughter's Dog

Our daughter has moved up north,
taken her Golden Retriever with her.
From the porch, we don't hear
the crunch of gravel under tires
or look up to the red gleam
of her Jeep arriving.

Tomorrow morning, we won't hear
the brisk scatter of leaves
beneath four feet
and a snuffling nose.
And we won't spy, above the shrubs,
Roscoe's resplendent plume

held high, on a mission to find
what had been here but now is not.

Real

The closest I've been to a grey fox
is on South Congress Avenue.
He stares glassy-eyed
at encased costume jewelry, a Pinocchio
puppet, *a Rare 1930's*
Red Riding Hood Toothbrush Holder.

Price-reduced but with tail erect
and in mid-stride,
Grey Fox (on Astroturf!) shares plastic
grass with a six-inch *Large Croc Head.*
I stroke the fox the way

my young daughter stroked the mule deer
head displayed on her grandfather's wall,
her father lifting her
to touch the deer's nose
once wet and shiny in sunlight.

Back on the floor, she ran
to the adjacent room looking
for the animal's body
on that side of the wall,
the family amused by her confusion.

My husband hunts for an old camera
in the display case on the shelf
with an embossed crocodile purse.
The metal on the camera body gleams
but he tells me the insides are not
in working order.

Calves

Up ahead
a dusty pickup
pulls a blue
livestock trailer
loaded with calves.
They jostle
and stumble.
The afternoon
is indifferent
to their discomfort.
Between rusted bars
a frantic eye
peers.

Sunday Afternoon in Texas

Not far away, unconcerned with us, a long
gray snake slides across the shade garden.
In Afghanistan, it is dark and bombs are falling.
Here the sky is clear, humidity low. A rare day.

We eat an October lunch under the trees —
roast pork with spaetzle and rotkraut, icy beer,
pumpernickel thick and sweet as cake — reminding
us of when we were stationed in Germany.

On a Sunday afternoon, we drove
to nearby Hohenzollern Castle.
In my mind a photo from that day.
Grant, little and grinning astride a cannon.

Before lunch, a television reporter said
it's been a month since the towers fell.
It hardly seems a month, I think,
then remember how time, winding

its way through our lives
after our son died, felt like yesterday
and years ago at the same time.

Laura Quinn Guidry

A Handout

A woman approaches me
at the gas pump, apologizes, then asks
if I can spare a couple of dollars,
says her child is sick and her car's out of gas.

She's driven all the way from Giddings
(asks if I know where Giddings is)
on her way to the Children's Hospital
a few more miles down the street.

I dig in my purse, put ten dollars in her hand.
She thanks me, asks God to bless me.
Later, I wonder if I gave her the money
because I believed she had a sick child

or because Giddings is the town
just down the highway from where I live
or because the day looked bright,
but around us, darkness always hovers.

Full Moon in Transom

She wanted to sleep beneath darkness
so she pulled down the shades
and lay on top of the bed covers.

But the sky is never still.
In the night, the moon moves
into the transom.

Its fullness enters the room.
Light finds her, floats over her.
Inevitable light.

Laura Quinn Guidry

The Snarl

The two grey foxes reappear at dusk.
They come for water from the makeshift
fountain and scraps of fruit we leave for them.
They know people live in the house

but knowing does not disturb their coming.
These two are likely from last spring's litter.
This is the month the mother would've
snarled and sent them away.

Drought has drained life from the pond.
Evergreens have turned brown, brittle.
Not far away, wildfires rage.
We sniff the air for smoke.

Mother has bared her teeth.

Thirst

    I wish I'd set out this tin
    bucket to catch all
    the moments that rained
    down, then ran
    off in rivulets or the sun burned
    away before they'd had
    a chance to soak into the ground.

    If I'd thought to do that then,
    now I could reach
    down with this knocked-about
    metal cup and bring up a sip.
    It would taste of gladness.

Laura Quinn Guidry

Under a Full Moon

the oaks' bare branches cast
shadows on the ground.

The bare earth is like skin
and the stark shadows, veins
through which darkness flows.

As if the night has turned itself inside out.

A good moon for hunting.
The hidden revealed.
The bloodbeat of impulse.

Looking out my bedroom window
wanting and not wanting to see.
The wintry world in a different light.

That strange glow.

Night is filled with contradictions.
The body, too — its longings,
the thoughts that course through it.

Odd to be old and full of desire.

Visitor

When I raise the window shade
a grey fox, the color of morning,
ambles away. Rain comes down hard
after five months. Thunder cracks.
Clocks flash. A window leaks.
We mop up with towels, retire
to the den to watch a video.
Rain pelts the metal roof, eases.
Stop the movie, you say. *Come see this.*

A pileated woodpecker has landed
in the oak closest to the house.
Uncommon, wary bird, big as a crow,
back as black, crested with red feathers
tall and thick like hair. White-faced,
the black line off its eye is like a mask,
the line off the base of its bill
turns downward as in a grimace.
A jester, a mad clown.

Not exactly pretty, you remark.
Better than pretty, I say.
The bird ratchets the tree
and is gone. Its call rises
to a wild laugh. Then, in the clearing,
we see the wide, white underwing
gleaming like the moon
beneath storm clouds.

Doors

Following him through dreams
she came so close once
in doors revolving around
the two of them.
He just ahead.
A single pane of glass between.
In the morning, she remembered
her palm pressed against
the cool rebuff of glass
and those doors,
how they turned.

Sign of Contradiction

> *Francis of Assisi walked at right angles*
> *to all that characterized his age.*
> *He was a sign of contradiction.*
>   — Mother Francis, PCC, Abbess
>   Monastery of Our Lady of Guadalupe

The dog and I meander about campus on our early walk.
My morning ponderings as rambling as our path.
An insistent thought at the periphery.

A Franciscan sister walks the second story breezeway
between university buildings,
her head bent over the papers she is reading.

She is a silhouette, tall and purposeful, framed
for an instant by the black pillars and railing,
the symmetry of lampposts lined up

along the sidewalk below, and in the distance,
the street, parked cars, tunnel of trees.
I wonder what she is reading.

Morning is heavy and still.
Light from the lamps a contained glow.
The dog and I wander onto the grounds

of the Rothko Chapel in the quiet neighborhood.
Houses on both sides of The Menil painted
grey and white like the museum.

I might like to live in one of those houses.
At my age, I'm immobilized by choices:
the gravity of *for the rest of my life.*

Laura Quinn Guidry

On the way back, our path meets the sister's.
At ground level, she is no taller than I am.
Below her brown habit, dirty white walking shoes.

She turns onto the quadrangle and continues —
a rhythmic following in footsteps —
while I, envy-ridden, head home.

Flash Flood

All-afternoon rain floods Friday rush hour
streets in Houston. Suddenly, I'm driving
through too-deep water. I turn onto a side street,
end up in the parking lot of a restaurant,
grab my umbrella, a copy of *The Moviegoer* —
a book I should have read years ago —
and dash inside.

The hour turns happy. A glass of Pinot gris,
crusty bread, cold butter. The windows
fog up, as they do in New Orleans
during a summer rain. New Orleans — the setting
of the book and where I grew up.
The familiarity of Gentilly, the long streets
named Elysian Fields and Chef Menteur.

I remember wanting my parents to buy
the white cottage we saw in Gentilly
on our house hunting trip, but they didn't.
I wanted to move in there
because of the two regal, white concrete dogs
that flanked the entrance like stone lions,
vainly safeguarding home.

Laura Quinn Guidry

His Dog

The man and woman watch news coverage of rising waters in the city that once was home and see the dogs the owners couldn't take with them. The dogs bark, partly in desperation, partly in protection of what is slipping away. Other owners stayed because they wouldn't abandon their dogs. *Would you have left Charlie?* she asks him. *No way,* he says. She doesn't doubt him. He loves that dog the way a new mother loves her baby. Because he is much alone in the world and the dog's world turns upon his comings and goings. There is a fierceness to that kind of love. But because the man is older, a sadness, too—for what was lost and for the dog's blind trust and for the things he understands about the world and himself that the dog cannot.

Flavor

On an avenue in a hard-hit area
we seek out the old sno ball stand.
The name is on a corner of the building
but the building is gutted.
In the parking lot, there's a new metal stand.

The girl at the window says it's not the same
owner but the flavors are the same.
No, they're not, I tell her,
There's no red cream (and cream)
remembering that flavor you couldn't quite place,

paper cones and wooden spoons,
Ortolano Sno Wizard transforming chunks of ice
into finely-shaved mounds, syrup poured in layers
so the flavor soaked all the way through,
evaporated milk (cream) drizzled across the top.

Once a handwritten board overflowed with flavors.
Now there are fewer — and only the predictable ones.
I order dreamsicle, ask about the cream.
It's already mixed in, she says.
Nearby, one old man is telling another where

the best sno ball stands in New Orleans used to be,
his favorite one uptown.
He leans into his one-way conversation,
gesturing, speaking loudly,
his lips and tongue stained bubble gum blue.

Laura Quinn Guidry

Tommy

A boy I knew
when I was thirteen

had dark hair
and dreamy eyes.

All the girls
had a crush on him.

His younger brother got killed
in a hunting accident.

What did we know
of death, then?

What did we know
of life?

At the church
Tommy looked stunned.

We girls sat on the pew
looking pretty. Hoping.

A Few Words

I must learn to love this place again.
Once, I loved its distance from the city,
its bordering on wildness,
the way the old roses tangle and spill over stones.
I loved the laden silences and night noise,
nights so dark the farthest stars reveal their fire.

But when the coyote boldly
appears in our yard at dusk and dawn
and when, a few feet
from the front porch, the copperhead
sinks its fangs into the neck of our spaniel,
everything changes.

I must learn to love the world again.
The hard, unbounded world.
I have only a few words and some images.
Yesterday, the dog that bolted from its yard
to charge a car, and was struck.
Its strange gyration of adrenalin, pain
and bewilderment.

I want to blot out that image
and others. Still, I summon them.

Laura Quinn Guidry

Reckoning the Earth

Have you reckoned a thousand acres much?
Have you reckoned the earth much?
— Walt Whitman

Now when we sit on this hilltop, a clump of shrubs
mars our view of a thousand acres beyond the fence.
In the fifteen years since we set the bench here

we've glimpsed deer in the clearing at first light
and coyotes by the edge of the woods near nightfall.
Sometimes even the exotic appeared — an ostrich,

survivor of some failed venture, a fad.
Once two cows lay dead side by side in the field,
the herd grazing nearby.

Two turkey buzzards perched
atop the carcasses. The rest of the scavengers
crowded around — like a scene from the Serengeti.

We want what we had back.
Mist clinging to grass until midday.
Cattle drifting toward the fence in late afternoon

predictable as clockwork.
A truck unloading hay, the cows' circling.
Night seeping through the trees into the field.

It's not row upon row of look-alike houses,
what we've feared coming, that spoils the vista —
the old farmer is still alive, his land intact.

It's that overgrown underbrush,
drought-tolerant and tenacious,
now crowding out the sky.

As if the world gave us an open field,
an abundance — we who were eager to disappear —
then, took it back.

III

Incandescent

At four a.m., we're on our deck looking up
at a meteor shower. You're leaning back
in the Adirondack chair, claiming the view from
there is good enough. I'm leaning back against
the corner railing, craning to see all the sky I can,
like a child not wanting to miss anything.

Streaks of light appear every few seconds
but we never know where.
It's kind of like fishing, you comment.
We point and say things such as,
Look at that one, That's a good one
or *A really big one.*

After a while, tired, we go back to bed.
*It's not as if there's a grand finale to
wait for,* I remark. This is the real thing.
Almost instantly, you are sleeping.
I still watch the sky, from my window now.

This is my favorite place in the house —
our bed, this window I look out of
from our bed, the way it frames the silhouettes
of the cedars, their varying heights making a "v"
in the sky where the stars drift in and the moon
comes sometimes but doesn't stay.

If when we die, we can choose
our pathway to the light,
I'd like to fly right out this window
up above the cedars, over the pond, placid
in moonlight, up through the sky
higher and higher to where the stars are.

I'd like to see our son again and my mother

and father. Do you think they wait for us?
Or are our lives like the star that just burst
through the opening of trees, trailing light,
a glimmer in my little piece of sky?
Is that enough, love? Is that enough?

Bird of Many Colors

Splendor on a branch of a withered oak.
A small bird—scarlet, iridescent blue,
yellow-green—sends me
leafing through the bird book for a name.

"Painted Bunting.
The most gaudily colored American bird."
What was light is now laden with words.
What was just here is now gone.

Remember when there couldn't be too much color?
A big sheet of drawing paper.
A box of crayons—64 count. The crayons' names,
a rich roll of the tongue, a mysterious invitation.

Now I trace a word back to its beginnings—
"gaud from the Latin *gaudere*—to rejoice."
Remember when all of it—seeing,
imagining, making—was about joy.

Familiar

Today the ordinary returns.
Glass-topped table back beside chair.
Cup of coffee and book of poems within reach.
Fragile objects come down from upper shelves.
Sharp objects go back into lower drawers.

The family has gone home.
Our daughter called to say our grandson
beamed to see his playpen and toys
and squealed with delight
at the sight of his walker.

Now, in a quiet room, I read a poem,
then read it again.
Yesterday's rhymes but an echo—
soothing repetition, a baby's babble,
anticipation and pleasure of words.

Of Home

For weeks I've been entranced by a story.
Now I'm in the chapter that bears
the same name as the book.
No doubt important.
Something will be revealed.

But the scene the author creates—
three characters lying in the grass
on a clear summer evening
looking up at the stars—
transports me out of the story.

It's not the stars that interpose,
visible from the deck of my house
on this rocky hillside,
the constellations as sketchy here as there,
but the grass, the cradle of grass.

I've lived for years amid prairie grass
and prickly pear. Now this longing
for a verdant landscape, a lush lawn,
the taken-for-granted grass of my youth—
I can't find my way back into the story.

Sunset on the River from the 16th Floor

The sun has cast the river pink.
Brick buildings, too, have taken on the tint
of sundown. Even the rusted flues on rooftops flare.

Facades layered with faded, cracking paint
reveal past lives — *Sam Ball & Son*,
Buster Brown Hosiery.

Along streets below, building blocks of color —
cream, salmon, apricot, apple green —
like rows of produce filling the French Market.

Water color melds from smoky pink to blue-note grey.
At day's end, a procession of tugboats pushing barges.
A dredge spews dark hillocks of silt.

Now lights come on across the river.
Buildings on the west bank cast rectangular
reflections, like twin cities of land and water.

The moon, veiled in a shroud of clouds, drifts
in and out on the lazy lap of water.
Time, like the river, floats, bends.

Of the Grandfather I Barely Knew

I was too young to remember,
my father said. Though it was all
just as I said and me, only three.
The backyard of our new house
on the outskirts of Baton Rouge.
Friendly horses
within the neighbor's fence.
Behind the house, woods, dark
and friendly, too.

Early mornings my grandfather
and I sit on a low brick wall
out back.
We look into the woods.
There is silence between us,
peaceful silence —
a place I've been trying
to come back to
all my life.

Friday

From the sun's showy descent
oil slicks on the highway burn smoky pink.
I travel west from Houston
turn onto the gravel road
roll down the window
breathe deeply
drive slowly
past the line of darkening trees
the red, rusted shed
the field of golden coreopsis
and lavender thistle.

The sun on my left now and almost gone
I travel the rise of road
too late to see the longhorns
but in time for the two black horses
on the rim of the hill
shining blue against the last arc of day.

Here the road veers right.
If you look down the long gorge
you can see the buildings in Dime Box.
Following the curve of earth, I continue.
See how the trees are taking back
their shadows. A light wind ripples
the stillness. Inside the fence, someone
has stacked stones into three pyramids.
Cairns marking the setting sun, our path.
Listen, you can hear them.

This is where the road takes me.
This is what the wind tells me.
This is the hymn of the stones.

Laura Quinn Guidry

Heron

An odd plodding in the dry leaves
deep within the thicket.
At the edge of the porch, I listen and wait.

A great blue heron ascends!
Lumbering, aloft
but not belonging to the sky.

For a week last summer
the heron appeared on the berm of the pond.
Distant and vigilant.

In a week I will drive to the cemetery.
My son gone, one more year.
The meager flowers, the trip by rote.

Days when I watch from my window
I'd like to remember the heron,
the color of ash.

How it labored just now,
then lifted, recovering sky.

The Prairie Iris

A small thing surprises.
A slender stem in a field.

A purple flower,
purple of all the griefs
the heart has held.

Tender flower, half-hidden
in the buffalo grass,
did the gods send you?

It is impossible to live here lost.

Between Two Gardens

It is always dark when we enter.
Cool earth dark by day here
where oaks and cedars weave a canopy,
lichen encrusts rocks
in spongy shades of greens and grays.
When the moon rises
quicksilver creatures will come out.
A white stone marks the place where
we buried the ashes of our dalmatian Gypsy.
From a stone terrace
we see the other garden
where I planted fairy rose next to
prickly pear in the sunlight.
April, ardent in yellow, pink and clear blue.
In the corridor between two gardens
where wind blows
we hang three small temple bells in a tree.
We're weary from work and the time of year,
content to find a branch
the wind can swing
and gently ring the little bells.

The Hum

The star in its brilliance hovers in the distance the way the hummingbird hovered in nearness at dusk.
The vibration that fixes the star fastened the bird in the air so near the woman.
The green in the woman's shirt is the green that shimmered in the bird and that the star suggests.
The red in her shirt is the red of the flowers and the red of the star.
The tremble in the heart is the quiver in the wings and the pulse in the star.
The tip of the pen, dipped in ink, is the black-needled bill of the hummingbird.

Mimicry

I wake to a strange sound
when the moon
wrapped in swirling clouds
sheds no light.
A cry scrapes the door
ignores a wall.
Not a yip or a sad bay.
More a series of squawks
a night bird might make,
its raspy repetition
oddly melodic.

Grey fox now at my bedside,
I stroke his fur,
coarse and bristly.
He lies down like a dog
but he is not a dog.
The dark eyes bright,
smile, sleek as a blade.
His cry mimics other creatures'
as a gust of wind will turn
night noise into voices.

Turning

My mother, already dead,
could not be with me
when Grant died.
She came later
at night
to get me moving.
Not the keep-busy kind of moving
of unsolicited suggestion
so like the vertiginous flurry of activity
that had been my life
but the first kind.
Of beginning
and beginning again.

I can't say where she led me
only it was vast and dark.
Everywhere and nowhere.
We moved in a slow circle
and were not alone.
Other people and animals there, too.
It was as if we weren't moving at all.
All of space was moving
and we with it.
Turning.
And a togetherness of things.
A kindness.
Yes, a kindness encompassing us.

Language moves.
A cadence remembered,
breathed in and out.
Words hum and hush
sitting, rocking
standing, swaying.
Little moons becoming full
turning in perpetuity.

Laura Quinn Guidry

Frogs at the Robert Frost Farm

> *Spring is the mischief in me...*
> — Robert Frost, "Mending Wall"

In Derry, New Hampshire, frogs in the pond
near the absent mending wall
delight my grandsons. Better than animals
hiding in picture books. Bullfrogs
with bright green heads disappear
in duckweed. Dark spots on pickerel frogs
blend with dappled leaves on the water.

Earlier, the boys, restless, took
a "botanizing walk" through the fields
and woods with their mother
and grandfather, while I toured the house
and barn. A hundred years ago, Frost wrote
of the Hyla breed of frogs, whose silvery
voices like bells in the trees, announced spring.
Today we count fourteen pond frogs.

Now a pickerel frog, invisible in the shadows
a moment before, leaps.
My two-year-old grandson, following
his older brother's lead, reaches out with
one finger to touch the slick back of a bullfrog.
The frog is first to jump.
Oh, just another kind of outdoor game...

At Breakfast

Sitting at the breakfast table,
the sun illuminating the grain
in the wood, I look out the window

on a day becoming beautiful.
It reminds me of Grant—
how he seldom let beautiful days

slip past unnoticed.
A game of golf on his last.
A fishing trip planned for the next.

At the table, all these years of days
later, I am mindful of how the cream
mellows the strong coffee

and the kiwi marmalade on the wheat
toast satisfies, its singular sweetness
lasting after the bitter is gone.

Laura Quinn Guidry

Matrix

1. Koren[1]

I feel old at twenty, Koren told me,
after her brother died and she went back
to college, the other girls talking about
where they were going on Saturday night
and what they were going to wear.

I think of the girls still picking
wildflowers in the meadow by the lake—
not in the vale of Enna
but in the Texas hill country where
wild lilies are creamy-white crow poison.
And violet is the color of the blossoms
on silverleaf nightshade.

Recall the myth of Kore, daughter of Ceres,
goddess of the earth and growing things.
She was gathering flowers with her friends
when the god of the underworld
carried her away.

You are *old, now, sweetheart*, I answer
my daughter. Flowers drop, bower
abandoned, the wild vines will thrive—
greenbriar with its sharp spines; snailseed,
poisonous fruit of the moonseed family
and wild morning glory, its rosy petals
and dark center.

---

[1] Koren, *Kore* (Greek) "maiden"

2. Cornucopia

On Thanksgiving we're in Koren's kitchen,
her first holiday as hostess, her fiancé basting
the turkey, her grandmother putting the dirty rice
with its plump oysters into the oven.
Our voices fill the small room.

A ripe pomegranate soaks in the sink.
Reaching into the cool water, Koren parts
the scored fruit. Rind and pith float.
Crimson seeds descend. She scoops them up
to sprinkle on the salad.

I remember when the earth didn't yield abundance.
Ceres, consumed by grief, cursed the ground
she would later enter to retrieve her daughter.
But that part about the pomegranate —
the maiden having tasted the sweet seeds...

What are the rules for reentering life?
Ceres compromised. The Fates decreed —
Kore, having eaten forbidden fruit,
would divide her time between the light
and the dark, forever to traverse two worlds.

We have things to thank the gods for today.
But to this world of plenty, I avow:
I can't come all the way back.
I won't come all the way back.
Don't ask it.

3. Imprint

My daughter is older now, married,
living in a city far from here.
We talk on weekends.

She is a printmaker, working with
matrices of wood, stone, metals.
Our common ground–ink on paper.

Koren calls from her studio.
She is making an intaglio print.
She describes the process —

the image is incised below the surface.
I try to visualize how
the ink seeks the deepest cut.

4. Matrix

The Greeks understood the power
of symbol to sustain us.

At Eleusis, a great mystery grew up
around the mother-daughter goddess.

She is seed corn yielding to the dark earth
and reaped corn.

She is virgin earth
and virgin mother.

She is genetrix of all things
and matrix to which all things return.

She is Tellus Mater, Magna Mater
and Mater Dolorosa.

She is the night
and the new moon.

A Song for Listeners

Koren is studying Buddhism.
She has had a glimpse of reality.
She still calls sometimes to talk
about the everyday—a decision
to make, a frustration to vent.
I like those times.

But even better
are the times when I listen—
she, now the teacher.
Don't mothers want more
for their children than for themselves?

I read Huxley's *The Perennial Philosophy*,
Huston Smith's *Forgotten Truth*
but her knowing is first-hand.
Outside, a Carolina wren is perched
on the porch swing,
singing its little heart out.

Thanks

My gratitude to Pamela Booton and Lowell Mick White of Alamo Bay Press.

Thank you to Sally Ridgway, mentor and friend, for critiquing my poems through the years and reading my manuscript. Thanks to my old friend and classmate from New Orleans, Ken Fontenot, for his insights on my manuscript. And a deep appreciation to Roberto Bonazzi for his inspiration and support.

Thanks to my friend Sybil Estess, with whom I started a poetry group in Houston fifteen years ago. And thanks to members of this group for their thoughtful critiques: Kelly Patton, Vivian Macias, Dom Zuccone, Varsha Shah, the late Martha Weathers and many others who were a part of the group at different times.

And a special thanks to Larry, my husband of forty-nine years and the final critic of my poems.

Acknowledgments

Acknowledgment and appreciation to the editors of the publications in which these poems appeared, some in a slightly different form.

Big Land, Big Sky, Big Hair: Best of the Texas Poetry Calendar: "Fridays"

Cinco de VIA: Five Years of Poetry on the Move: "Calves"

Concho River Review: "A Handout" and "Alone"

damselfly press: "At Breakfast"

descant: "Under A Full Moon"

Down to the Dark River: Contemporary Poems about the Mississippi River: "Sunset on the River from the Sixteenth Floor"

Earth's Daughters: "Flight"

In the Eye: A Collection of Writings: "Fishing with My Father"

In These Latitudes: Ten Contemporary Poets: "A Few Words", "Alone," and "Love Poem"

Louisiana Literature: "Incandescent," "Red," and "Skin"

San Antonio Express-News: "Bird of Many Colors"

Shadow and Light: A Literary Anthology on Memory: "Turning"

Texas Poetry Calendar: "Before Dawn," "Fridays,"

"The Prairie Iris," and "Visitor"

Texas Weather: "The Snarl," "Thirst," and "Visitor"

The Paddle Wheeler: "Flash Flood," "So Damn Hot," "Of Home," "The Snarl," and "That Little Girl"

The Southern Poetry Anthology Vol. VIII: Texas: "Alone"

The Texas Review: "Mother Oaks"

Untameable City: Poems on the Nature of Houston: "Sign of Contradiction"

Voices from the Porch: "Our Daughter's Dog"

The Weight of Addition: An Anthology of Texas Poetry: "Rush"

We Never Walk Alone: "Listening"

Women's Journal: "Heron"

About Laura Quinn Guidry

Laura Quinn Guidry was born in Baton Rouge, Louisiana, and grew up in New Orleans. She has lived in Texas for thirty-six years. Laura began writing poetry after the sudden death from heart disease of her son Grant when he was twenty-four. She published her first poem at age fifty-two.

Her work has appeared in numerous journals, including *Concho River Review*, *The Texas Review*, *Louisiana Literature*, and *descant*. She has been a four-time contributor to the *Texas Poetry Calendar*. Additionally, her work has been published in the *San Antonio Express-News,* and she was a featured poet at Poetry on the Move in San Antonio in 2012. Her poems have also appeared in numerous anthologies and a collection of her poems is in *In These Latitudes: Ten Contemporary Poets*.

Laura worked in health care administration for over twenty years at the Texas Medical Center in Houston. She and her husband Larry retired to Carmine, Texas, where they enjoy a quiet life in the country. Their daughter, Koren, and her husband, Chris, have two sons, Brenden and Nathan. Laura coordinates literary events at the Round Top Family Library.

Praise for the Writing of

Laura Quinn Guidry

A native of New Orleans, with deep roots in south and central Louisiana, **Laura Quinn Guidry** lived and worked as a healthcare administrator in Houston for years. Then tragedy changed her life and her amazing poems began. Grief and Gratitude are the "two gardens" this poet moves between. From her home now in Carmine, Texas, Laura writes in what she calls her "treetop writing retreat." One can find her there most any day, noticing birds, foxes, coyotes, even snakes. All of these creatures appear in her second garden, which is truly a delightful place to visit in person, or in her incredible, imagistic and metaphoric poems. Laura is now one of the very best "new" poets in the state of Texas, though she both writes and publishes far beyond our largest state's borders. This is her first full-length volume.
    —Sybil Pittman Estess, author of *Like That* and *Seeing the Desert Green*

Laura Quinn Guidry's poems ricochet off each other, multiplying resonance in their plurality, and the entire collection feels like a story, a narrative of the child who stayed and the child who left, but even in his clear leaving, he is still here, almost a ghost-spirit, a son-spirit. The poet steeps the final section in the mythic, and the book is elevated in profundity there; though grounded in reality, this section leaps into the timeless, the lessons we learn from the culmination of the real world and the other-world, the present world and the after-world. Inside this book resides the life of a woman who holds the real and the mythic in the balance of one body, locating it between mourning and memory, between the one who stayed and the one who left, lighting up the pages.
    —Marian Haddad, author of *Somewhere Between Mexico and a River Called Home* and *Wildflower. Stone.*